Butterflies
and Butterfly Gardening
IN THE PACIFIC NORTHWEST

Butterflies

and Butterfly Gardening

IN THE PACIFIC NORTHWEST

MARY KATE WOODWARD

whitecap

Edited by Ian Whitelaw
Proofread by Nelles Hamilton
Interior design by Christine Toller and Marjolein Visser
Drawings by Mary Kate Woodward
Photographs by Ian Lane, Richard Beard, Per Joensen, Mary Kate Woodward, Cris Guppy,
    Gwen and Paul Odermatt, Dana Visalli

Printed and bound in Canada by Friesens.

Library and Archives Canada Cataloguing in Publication
Woodward, Mary Kate
    Butterflies and butterfly gardening in the Pacific Northwest / Mary Kate Woodward.
    ISBN 1-55285-707-7
    1. Butterfly gardening—Northwest, Pacific. I. Title.
QL544.6.W66 2005   638'.5789'09795   C2005-900613-7

The publisher acknowledges the financial support of the Government of Canada through the Book Publishing Industry Development Program for our publishing activities.

*This book is dedicated to my father, who taught me
to love wild creatures. I gratefully acknowledge the help
and support of my husband and the generosity of those who shared their
photographs. A special thank you is due to Cris Guppy
for his invaluable assistance.*

Contents

Introduction   9

Essentials of Planning a Butterfly Garden   11

The Butterfly Landscape   15

Larvae: Famished Feeders   23

Flowers: A Garden Tapestry   26

Favourable Features   36

Relax, Observe, Enjoy   39

A Gallery of Butterflies   41

Climate Zone Map   84

Larval Host Plants   86

Food Sources for Adult Butterflies   88

Sources of Plants and Seeds   99

Glossary   103

Index of Common Names   104

Anise Swallowtail larvae

Introduction

Creating butterfly refuges in urban backyards may help offset the habitat destruction perpetrated by the human race on these beautiful insects. A successful urban butterfly garden will provide larval and adult food plantings, as well as flat rocks and mud puddles in a sunny, wind-free location. Butterflies requiring wooded or other specialized habitats may be enticed into your garden by the inclusion of a few of their favourite trees or features.

It is not difficult to create a butterfly preserve. One must simply adopt an attitude and approach to gardening that prioritizes the needs and likes of butterflies over those of humans. In fact, the two are not totally incompatible. Butterfly gardens and people gardens can exist in parallel with a few modifications on our part.

Annuals such as nasturtiums provide a season-long colour pattern to attract butterflies to your garden. Mixing annuals among clumps of perennials will enhance your garden's colour brilliance and extend its flowering season.

Essentials of Planning a Butterfly Garden

Start with what you have. Take an inventory of your existing landscape. If you live in an older urban residential area, you probably already have a number of useful plants or butterfly-attracting features in your garden. Some good features to look for include trees on which caterpillars feed, flowering hedges, ornamental shrubs such as lilac and firethorn, bird baths, stone walls, perennial flower beds and borders, as well as "weed" patches. You may find all you need to do is concentrate masses of flowering plants, add larval hosts, and alter your attitude to weeds and the use of chemicals in gardening.

Never use pesticides or herbicides. These kill multitudes of desirable insects, such as butterflies, as quickly as the few pests they are intended to control. Many of the caterpillars seen munching a few leaves today are tomorrow's butterflies. Eliminating these butterfly larvae also eliminates the beautiful butterflies one wants to see flitting about one's garden. If your cabbages are at risk from Cabbage White butterflies and their larvae, plant lure-plants like nasturtium nearby to attract egg-laying butterflies away. Also, or alternatively, plant strongly scented onions, thyme, or wormwood beside your cabbage-family vegetables to help mask their attractive scent.

Working to grow a single plant species rather than encouraging species diversity within a garden area artificially limits which butterflies, if any, can use the planting. Lawns that include clovers, speedwell, tiny English daisies, and other weeds attract many butterflies. The popular golf-course green lawn, maintained by the use of pesticides and herbicides, is sterile and supports no butterflies.

I leave the grass uncut in the corners of my garden and set the lawn mower blade to avoid cutting grass too short. Flowering plants, including clovers, daisies, speedwell and yarrows, flower in the lawn, creating a multicoloured carpet attractive to butterflies.

No neat-freaks please. Avoid raking or disturbing a butterfly garden. Some butterflies and moths lay their eggs or overwinter as larvae or pupae on grasses, in leaf litter on the ground, or burrowed into the earth. The large, beautiful Sphinx moths are an example of a species whose caterpillars burrow into the ground to pupate. Digging in, cultivating, or raking up leaves and litter to tidy plantings destroys these butterfly and moth children, and therefore the next generation of adult butterflies and moths. Suppress your neat-freak tendencies if you want to attract butterflies and maintain a successful butterfly habitat.

Keeping butterfly gardens separated from playgrounds for children and pets is another consideration when planning such a garden. Playgrounds are incompatible with the undisturbed oases required by butterfly nurseries. It is also inadvisable to plant some of the best larval hosts beside pathways or areas frequented by bare-legged people. Plants such as stinging nettle are most unwelcoming to bare skin.

Clean (pesticide- and herbicide-free) undisturbed lawns and gardens encourage visits from butterflies.

Redefine the word "weed." Many weeds are choice food for both adult butterflies and their larvae. Weeds and parasitic plants are not bad plants. They are simply pieces in the giant jigsaw puzzle of Earth's ecology. Some are essential larval hosts for certain butterflies.

Common Woodnymph, underwing, on thistle. Saltspring Island, B.C.

For example, mistletoe, a parasitic plant vilified by the logging industry, is the sole larval host for some Hairstreak butterflies. The demise of mistletoe would mean the extinction of these butterflies. Stinging nettles are the favored larval host for numerous butterflies, and the sole host for some.

Observe which plants caterpillars congregate on. Often large numbers of caterpillars will chomp happily on plants that gardeners work hard to eliminate. Examples of these include thistles, stinging nettles, cow parsnips, clovers, vetches, and uncut grasses. Both caterpillars and adult butterflies frequent such weeds. A butterfly garden must include local butterflies' favourite plants instead of the traditional landscape favourites of human beings. A good compromise is to include those butterfly favourites one considers attractive in the visible landscape, while keeping others in hidden corners. Alternatively, a butterfly garden may be built in one area of a yard, like a separate room, while other areas serve other purposes or preferences.

Avoid human-caused butterfly hazards. Some butterfly hazards are natural, for example predators such as birds, dragonflies, and spiders and their webs. Others include migration for some species, the wind and weather, the butterflies' own often very short life spans, and the fragility of their bodies. However, other hazards are caused by humans, and many of these are unnatural and avoidable. They include pesticides and herbicides, the removal of so-called "weeds" (many of which are prime butterfly favourites or obligatory larval hosts), some farming, forestry, and industrial practices with their consequent habitat destruction, as well as human butterfly collectors. Hazards such as roadways and fast-moving vehicles claim millions of butterflies annually, as anyone who has cleaned a vehicle grill and headlights after a country drive will recognize. It is unreasonable to stop driving, but the huge number of butterflies killed on roadways is just another reason for assisting butterfly survival by creating butterfly-friendly habitats. Patches of weeds such as dandelions and thistles left in several places in my back garden and along the driveway have always been prime favourites of visiting butterflies, as well as some birds. People who do not like the appearance of these weeds can put them in unobtrusive corners, for example the space behind the compost or beside the garage or shed. Some weeds are happy secreted behind perennial garden beds or shrubbery. Others fit well right in the middle of a perennial border.

Butterfly and dragonfly on car grill

The Butterfly Landscape

To create an instant butterfly garden, start by determining which butterflies frequent your area. Then plant the larval hosts and favoured adult food plants of these species. Stinging nettle, which hosts the larvae of several large, colourful butterflies, is a good plant to begin with. A couple of weeks after you first notice the butterflies, search nearby back lanes, ditches, creek banks, and, with permission, friends' properties for caterpillars on host plants of the species you planted in your

Garden: Asclepias tuberosa, Echinacea purpurea

Monarch larva

own yard. Since caterpillars are easier to see than tiny butterfly eggs, beginners should watch for caterpillars. Lift plants with caterpillars on them or cut inhabited stems, carefully avoiding shaking the caterpillars off. (Be careful not to take anything from a park or nature conservation area.) Put the stems in water in a bottle and immediately transport the new tenants to your garden. Settle the bottle in the soil among similar growing specimens in your yard, and then watch the caterpillars migrate onto your plants. As caterpillars grow and fatten, watch for them to pupate. Not knowing the species of larvae collected, you won't know whether they will pupate above ground or below, or whether the adult will be a butterfly or a moth. Collect several different specimens and enjoy watching them grow into different adults.

Build an urban butterfly garden out of the wind (butterflies are delicate creatures, easily buffeted by air currents) and where it will receive plenty of sunshine. A sheltered southern exposure is a good choice. If possible, include a rock garden or stone wall. The large, brightly coloured butterflies most people want to attract to their gardens seek bright, warm, calm oases. They can be seen basking on concrete patios, on the stones of a rock wall, or along the edges and base of a bird bath where such garden features are available to provide them with quiet, undisturbed sunbathing.

A birdbath can be doubly attractive—supplying both a warm basking surface for butterflies and a damp area from which they can suck minerals and moisture.

Painted Lady, upperwing, sunning on concrete patio

Two good designs for butterfly gardens are a horseshoe-shaped planting and a layered island planting. Illustrations of both designs appear below and on the next page. Trees should be planted at the back of the horseshoe planting or in the center of the island planting. Shrubs should be next to the trees, and lower perennials and annuals should go on the outside of these shrubs. Both gardens benefit from being interplanted with annuals each year. Included in each garden design are a water source, in this case a birdbath, and a dry stone wall with a southern exposure for basking butterflies. The island design can be a simple circle or an irregular shape. The latter offers more edge area, which provides more space for butterfly attractions.

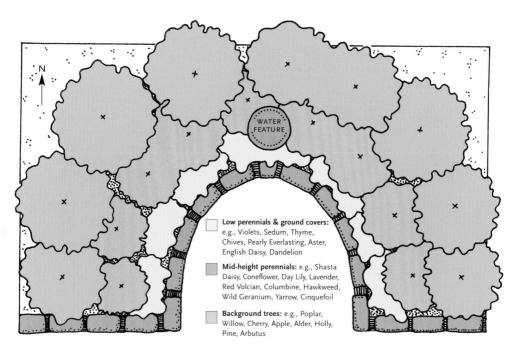

Low perennials & ground covers: e.g., Violets, Sedum, Thyme, Chives, Pearly Everlasting, Aster, English Daisy, Dandelion

Mid-height perennials: e.g., Shasta Daisy, Coneflower, Day Lily, Lavender, Red Volcian, Columbine, Hawkweed, Wild Geranium, Yarrow, Cinquefoil

Background trees: e.g., Poplar, Willow, Cherry, Apple, Alder, Holly, Pine, Arbutus

Horseshoe-shaped garden planting

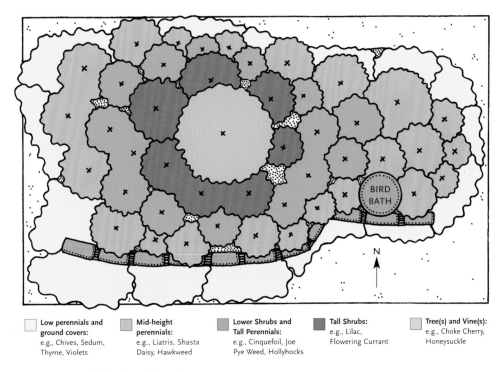

Low perennials and ground covers: e.g., Chives, Sedum, Thyme, Violets	Mid-height perennials: e.g., Liatris, Shasta Daisy, Hawkweed	Lower Shrubs and Tall Perennials: e.g., Cinquefoil, Joe Pye Weed, Hollyhocks	Tall Shrubs: e.g., Lilac, Flowering Currant	Tree(s) and Vine(s): e.g., Choke Cherry, Honeysuckle

Layered island garden planting

To create butterfly gardens like these, begin by choosing the best location. Mark out the size with stakes and lay a hose around the perimeter of the proposed garden bed to help visualize the finished shape. If you choose the horseshoe shape, be sure to point the opening of the horseshoe toward the south. Dig out the area, loosen the soil, and level the surface. Have the soil tested to discover what, if any, changes you need to create the appropriate soil texture and pH for the species you intend to plant. Place trees around the outer edge of the horseshoe-shaped garden or in the center of the island planting. Plant tall shrubs, such as buddleia and lilac, in front of the trees in the horseshoe, with the tallest at the back of the curve, or surrounding the trees if using the island design. Next, add a row of mid-height shrubs and tall herbacious perennials, such as Joe Pye Weed and hollyhocks. At the inside curve of the planting bed, or around the edge of the island, put shorter perennials and ground covers, such as pinks, violets, chives, and thyme. Take care to space plants with room to grow to their mature sizes. Any open spaces may be filled with annuals that will make the planting look full and lush even in its first year. Gardens planted in this manner are layered from tall trees down to the lowest groundcovers. This provides vertical as well as horizontal edges, including foliage and flowers at various heights to attract butterflies. Honeysuckle vines growing through my own shrubbery attract swallowtail butterflies as well as hummingbirds to their masses of yellow and pink flowers.

Such a planting is primarily intended to attract adult butterflies, but you will notice some plants that double as larval hosts. Examples include asters, which feed Crescent butterfly larvae; hollyhock, used by West Coast Lady caterpillars; thistle, eaten by Painted Lady larvae; and violets, the larval host of some Fritillaries. In the case of thistles, spent flower heads should be religiously snipped off and disposed of to maintain good relations with your neighbours, who may not appreciate an invasion by multitudes of tiny prickly plants.

The photograph below shows a butterfly, whose food preferences include moisture from the edges of mud puddles, sucking up moisture from a damp area on the base of a concrete water fountain.

Satyr Anglewing, underwing, feeding near water fountain.
Moberly, B.C.

Educate yourself. If you have time, observe your neighbourhood for a year before building your butterfly garden. Keep a diary of the butterflies you see, when you see them (which dates and times of day), where they are seen (on which plants or surfaces), and what they are doing. Discover which butterflies are most common and which are occasional visitors. You will notice there is a progression of species hatching as larvae, pupating, and emerging as adults, from the early Blues through late-season second or third generation Painted Ladies. Once you know which species you may reasonably expect to entice into your yard, you can plan your butterfly garden realistically. Plant the favored larval and adult food plants of the species you have observed and wish to attract. If some of these plants are plentiful in neighbouring yards, add varieties less commonly seen in your area. If you plant something a little unusual that is a butterfly favourite, you may entice a greater number and variety of butterflies to your garden. To maximize the numbers of butterflies visiting your garden, make sure the right plants are available when the butterflies who use them will be present in your neighbourhood.

Butterfly garden

Larvae:
Famished Feeders

Supply favored larval food sources for the caterpillars of butterflies as well as a selection of adult foods (which are usually different from the larval preferences) for various butterfly species. Often there is a choice of acceptable adult food sources. Some butterflies prefer the nectars of a variety of flowers; others like rotting fruit, or animal dung, or damp, boggy ground. However, many butterfly larvae are host-specific, tolerating little or no dietary variance. These butterflies will lay their eggs nowhere but on or near the appropriate larval host plant. Some examples of preferred larval hosts include trees such as alder, cottonwood, aspen, and willow, and perennials like cow parsnip, angelica, thistle, and stinging nettle, as well as wild cress, clover, and mistletoe.

Of course, few urban gardens can accommodate larval hosts for all the butterflies that might visit their location. Survey the neighbourhood to discover which larval hosts are already present nearby. Planting a number of absent or less-plentiful ones in your own garden increases the probability of attracting a greater variety of butterflies to the area and to your garden.

Red Admiral larva
< Milbert's Tortoiseshell larvae on stinging nettle

Plant two or three patches of each larval food plant in different locations around the garden. Many female butterflies lay only a few eggs on each of several leaves of the larval host, and then move to another plant or location. Having more than one clump of host plants offers her the safeguard of spreading her offspring over a wider area. This strategy protects such butterfly offspring from extermination should one plant or planting succumb to insectivores, parasites, weed- eaters, or other disasters of natural or human origin.

A choice planting I was growing as a border along my driveway was eradicated by a weed-eater when a good neighbor, thinking she was doing me a favor, tidied the driveway. Luckily, a few smaller clumps of the same weed were secreted in nooks and corners elsewhere in my garden. Since that event, I have kept the more public parts of my garden planted with species less likely to be labeled as weeds.

Milbert's Tortoiseshell larva

Be sure plant foods are available at the times the larvae and adults will be in the garden. Most butterflies are short-lived. Each year they arrive by migration or emerge from hibernation or pupae at approximately the same time or times in any given location. Some butterflies that appear to stay all summer, or whose populations peak more than once during the season, go through two or more generations (egg to larva to pupa to adult) each year. Multiple generations are most common in temperate and tropical climates. In the short, severe climate of the north, many butterflies manage only one generation per year. Some even take two years to complete their life cycle. Eggs are laid the first year, the species overwinters in the larval or pupal state, and then emerges as an adult in its second summer.

Butterfly eggs and larvae may be found on, and often under, the leaves of their larval hosts. Thus the butterfly's complete life cycle can sometimes be observed in one's own garden. This was the case with the West Coast Lady butterfly pictured here. It was one of three caterpillars discovered nibbling hollyhock leaves in August in my garden in B.C. It was photographed through all the stages of its development, emerging as a very hungry adult butterfly in September.

West Coast Lady, upperwing, basking on doghouse

Larvae grow quickly. They outgrow their skins and molt several times before they mature to transform into pupae. This series of molts separates growth periods called instars. Some caterpillars may be one colour during early instars and a completely different colour during their later instars.

Flowers:
A Garden Tapestry

Use masses of bloom. Design the garden using groups of perennial shrubs and flowers to create masses of bloom. Butterflies are attracted to large groupings of flowers, and a deep perennial border satisfies this need. Plant taller shrubs, such as lilac, honeysuckle, firethorn, red flowering currant, and buddleia, to the rear. These work as a windbreak, reducing air turbulence around the border. They also create a floral background. Flowering vines like honeysuckle may be planted to climb through these shrubs, thus expanding the flowering period and colour show of the background planting. In front of the tallest row of shrubs, plant mid-height shrubs, such as perennial fuchsia and potentilla, intermixed with tall perennial flowers, such as bee balm, columbine, and shasta daisies. Some of the shorter vining vetches may be grown through these. A layer of still lower growing flowers and herbs, such as oregano, sedums, chives, dandelion, hawkweeds, and English daisies, can be grown at the front edge of the planting. This is a compact and practical method of attracting many passing butterflies to stop for a meal.

Use single-flowering plant varieties. Their nectars are more accessible to butterflies than the newer, larger hybrid double blossoms and pompoms. Nectar pockets in the latter varieties, if they exist, may be out of a butterfly's reach. Hollyhocks, zinnias, marigolds, daisies, and roses are all examples of flowers available in single-flowering varieties as well as the currently more popular compound blooms. It may be necessary to search through a number of stores and catalogs to find the single-flowering plants. They are less often stocked in nurseries today and can be rather difficult to find. Seed-saver societies, flower societies

specializing in old-fashioned species, and gardening clubs are all good sources for some of the old beauties. Magazines such as *Gardens West* include a column of letters from people who are searching for a particular plant or who are willing to trade seeds, plants, and information.

I have found unusual nectar-producing plants while at garage sales. Surprised vendors of used household goods rarely refuse to share a cutting, a seed head, or even a seedling with an eccentric gardener.

Clouded Sulphur, underwing, on yellow hawkweed

Overlap flowering plant groups to avoid colour gaps as one group finishes flowering and another begins to bloom. Masses of colour are especially attractive to butterflies.

As groups of spring bulbs finish flowering, clumps of early perennials planted between them will expand to hide dying flowers and foliage. These are followed by early summer-blooming perennials such as sweet rockets, pinks, columbines, and daisies, plus herbs such as oregano and chives, then by later summer ones, for example phlox, until the garden's parade of colour is ended with late fall's asters, hawkweeds, and chrysanthemums. A series of pictures taken through the gardening season of areas planted in this way will show a continually changing, but constantly blooming, brocade of colour and design.

Sara's Orange Tip

Mix annuals among clumps of perennials to enhance colour brilliance and extend the flowering season. Annuals bloom for extended periods, often all through the gardening season, outlasting the perennials that bloom in sequence around them. With the tremendous selection of annual bedding plants available at nurseries every year, the choice of species and colour is almost limitless. There are plants of all sizes, heights, flower types, and growth habits, and many are good additions to a butterfly-attractive flower bed. Gaps between perennials, when filled with annuals such as marigold, nasturtium, and zinnia, provide constant butterfly attraction within the ever-changing garden landscape. Annuals provide a season-long colour pattern around which the shorter bloom periods of perennials create a changing background.

Choose yellow, purple, and pink flower colours—these are butterfly favourites. As you watch butterflies in your neighbourhood, you will observe which flowers and plants they prefer to visit. Often they will choose the pink, purple, or yellow coloured blooms over other colours present—even other colours of flowers on the same plant species in the same flower bed. Buddleia shrubs are available with flower colours in several shades of purple, as well as pink, yellow, and white. Honeysuckle vines offer flowers of cream, yellow, pink, and a variety of shades of red. Daisies, even white ones, frequently exhibit bright yellow centers, such as the shasta shown on the next page, supporting a nectaring Red Admiral butterfly.

The yellow buddleia shrub in my own garden attracts more butterflies than any other plant or feature. Several different kinds of butterflies may be seen nectaring on its flower heads at the same time.

Butterfly garden: iris, salvia, sweet william

Red Admiral, underwing, on Shasta daisy

Red Admiral, upper- and underwings, on Buddleia

Select scented flowers, which are particularly alluring to many butterflies. Old-fashioned flowers often have strong, beautiful fragrances. This is in contrast to newer varieties, many of which have little or no perfume. Smell the sweet fragrance of the butterfly bush (buddleia), so named for its attractiveness to butterflies. This bush can be covered with butterflies competing for its nectar. Lilacs are popular with butterflies whose proboscises are long enough to reach the nectar pockets at the bottom of their tubular flowers. Lilac bushes in my garden in Dawson Creek, B.C., were adopted by a Mourning Cloak butterfly that spent many hours each day for several weeks sipping nectar from their flowers. Strongly perfumed night-flowering stocks are very attractive to the nocturnal moths. Some flower perfumes that humans find pungent or offensive, butterflies and moths find irresistible. Firethorn flowers are an example of this. In spring, small blue butterflies flit eagerly from flower to flower over a firethorn hedge, probing each blossom for its nectar, while humans find the firethorn's perfume less than sweet.

Include night-blooming flowers for moths, most of which fly after dark when butterflies have settled in protected places to await tomorrow's sun. This is one reason moths are less often seen. They feed on night-blooming flowers, such as evening primrose and stocks, as well as many of the same flowers as butterflies. Different moths, like butterflies, visit various preferred food sources: single, sweetly scented flowers, fruits, or animal droppings. Like their butterfly cousins, moth larvae are choosy about their host plants. Tiger moth larvae, for instance, prefer butterfly weed, while Eyed Sphinx moth larvae eat fireweed. The common names of some sphinx moths derive from larval host plants, for example the Wild Cherry and the Apple Sphinx. Other moth names come from wing markings, such as that of the Eyed Sphinx with its eye spot on each hind wing. One of these was perched above a motel doorbell in Princeton, B.C., when we arrived at 4 a.m. to catch a few hours of sleep.

Eyed Sphinx moth

Clinging to a wall or tree, moths often disappear into their background. Many moths, invisible sitting still, have brightly colourful underwings so are as beautiful in flight as their butterfly relatives.

The large silk moths, almost six inches in wingspan, are spectacularly beautiful. Drawn to light, they will repeatedly bump into lit window panes at night or fly through open doorways into the light of a room. The silk moth pictured here flew into the house one May night as we were taking our dogs out. Confused, it bounced off lights until it was caught, photographed, and released back outside.

Silk Moth

Control invasive plants. Some butterfly staples, such as mints and stinging nettles, have invasive tendencies. To prevent these plants from taking over, to the exasperation of the gardener and the disadvantage of nearby plants with less expansive habits, it is advisable to sink them in the garden in containers. Other aggressive favourites requiring careful containment include members of the blackberry family, such as my tayberry. Every few years, at the height of its bloom, flocks of Painted Lady butterflies on their northward migration descend on it in a fluttering cloud of colour. To entice some of them to stay and lay their eggs, I keep healthy thistles scattered in out-of-the-way places. I hope enough little caterpillars hatch in unobtrusive corners to allow some to survive the hazards of their species and mature to decorate my garden with their next generation of butterflies.

Some trees that are important as larval hosts can also be invasive. Willows are a problem if planted close to a building, as their roots encroach on drains. Such trees should be planted away from one's house, preferably near a creek or ditch that will attract their roots.

Painted Lady, underwing, on tayberry

Favourable Features

Consider the borrowed landscape. Cooperate with a neighbour or neighbours to supply some of the larger shrubs and trees required by butterflies like Admirals, Mourning Cloaks, and Swallowtails. A number of their favored plants are probably already thriving nearby. It may only be necessary to add variety and some specific larval host requirements. Once these trees become fixtures in the garden and the butterflies have found them, they will return to them again and again. Of course, the chance that butterflies will choose larval plantings in any given back yard is related to the numbers of larval hosts, as well as the numbers of butterflies of that species in the neighbourhood.

A Mourning Cloak will often take possession of a favourite perch on a tree branch overlooking its chosen territory. It will return to this same spot regularly between periods of feeding or patrolling its territory. The tree is not necessarily the butterfly's larval host. Any tree with a conveniently placed, partly exposed branch near a good food source and an area where the butterfly can patrol in search of a mate is acceptable.

A branch of a cottonwood tree beside my yard was the favourite perch of a possessive Mourning Cloak for a few weeks while the butterfly laid claim to the yard's lilacs. It chased other butterflies away and spent hours daily sipping nectar from the lilacs' flowers.

Provide flat basking rocks, since butterflies like to sunbathe to warm themselves. Patios, stone walls, large stepping stones, and

Mourning Cloak, upperwing, on wet gravel

concrete garden furniture, such as bird baths, as well as the warm siding on the south wall of a house or a piece of sun-bleached wood, are all welcomed as opportune basking sites.

Like other cold-blooded creatures, butterflies need to absorb warmth from their environment. Butterflies require this warmth to fly. They will sit, apparently luxuriating, on a warm rock or concrete surface absorbing the sun's heat, occasionally gracefully closing and opening their wings like a pair of brightly coloured fans. Watching them, you may observe them alternating between trips to nectar sources and to basking sites. Some will return to favourite basking sites repeatedly, giving a person wishing to photograph them opportunities to get good pictures. The Painted Lady shown on page 17 is one that returned again and again to my sunny concrete patio.

Create a muddy or boggy edge on a pond, or leave or create mud puddles for those butterflies, like some Blues, Swallowtails, and Sulphurs, known to gather on wet ground. When they are puddling, a group of brightly coloured butterflies with wings turned to the sunlight seems to move as if choreographed. Actually they are absorbing warmth from the sun while at the same time sucking up nutrients from the damp ground. They cannot swim, so they land on solid surfaces that are wet, rather than in the water of the adjacent puddle, pond, ditch, or birdbath.

Butterflies sitting on animal droppings are doing the same thing. They are absorbing nutrients from the droppings. Scat butterflies, such as White Admirals and Green Commas, can be seen exhibiting this behaviour. They are some of nature's scavengers, helping to clean up our environment.

Clodius Parnassian butterfly, Demonstration Forest, B.C.

Relax, Observe, Enjoy

Expect surprises. Planting a butterfly's favored food plants does not guarantee it will visit. If the species is not in the area, it will not find the garden. The most reliable results are achieved by planting favored foods of the butterflies (and their larvae) known to frequent a neighbourhood. The favourite plants of larvae that will eat several foods vary from area to area. Growing a selection of plants known to be used by a specified butterfly's larvae will help determine what is choice in any particular garden.

With some careful observation, you can begin to eliminate plants that prove less popular, and concentrate on planting several patches of those on which most of that kind of larvae are seen. Larvae that are host-specific simplify one's planting options.

A friend and I studiously searched miles of cow parsnip plants for Anise Swallowtail larvae in an area where we were assured they would be found on this plant. Not once did we see the larvae on cow parsnip. However, each time we came across an angelica plant it had many Anise Swallowtail larvae at different stages of development all over it. Angelica seemed to be the Anise Swallowtail larvae's favored late-season host in that area.

Be an armchair gardener. Note that many choice butterfly plants (for both larvae and adults) are small, allowing people with small gardens, patios, and even low balconies to attract these beautiful insects for their enjoyment. Often such plants are native or naturalize easily and require less maintenance (e.g., watering and protection from frost) than their imported cousins. Whether building a balcony, back yard, or large-scale multi-acre landscape, you will find many plants attractive to butterflies less expensive to acquire and support than the presently popular plantings of temperamental, often-imported specimens. Some of the latter are only marginally hardy, or must be treated as annuals in our north-of-tropical climates.

The creation of a butterfly garden can be a beautiful, low maintenance solution to landscaping. Such a garden is more interesting than most, with its "flying flowers" darting across the grass or hopping from blossom to blossom, and its many plant species less commonly included in urban gardens. Time saved on the care of finicky plants can be spent sitting in a favourite garden chair enjoying one's own floor show of butterflies and moths.

Painted Lady, upperwing, on zinnia

A Gallery of Butterflies

Observe the ingenious methods used by butterflies to protect themselves from environmental hazards. Bold designs or eye spots on the wings of some, like Swallowtails, lead predators to peck at wings, protecting the body and facilitating the butterfly's escape, missing only a notch from a wing. Others, like Anglewings, resemble dried leaves. One may almost step on such butterflies, unseen until they flit away, displaying previously hidden brightly coloured upperwing surfaces, just as a foot was about to descend upon them. Some, like the Monarch, wear bright orange wings signifying they are poisonous. Others copy the colours of poisonous butterflies, though they themselves are not toxic.

Monarch on zinnia

Larvae also display numerous methods of self-protection. They may resemble bird droppings, like Lorquin's Admiral larvae or, like Cabbage White larvae, be nearly invisible, mimicking a host plant's colours. Others wear colours indicating they are poisonous, display a foul-smelling osmeterium (a retractable stalk-like protruberance above the head) when disturbed, or exhibit large eye spots to scare or mislead predators. Still others drop to the ground to be lost in leaves beneath the larval host at the slightest disturbance of that host. Many cling to the bottoms of the leaves they eat, hidden to those who might be searching from above.

Butterflies age quickly. Their colours fade. Their wings become tattered or have chunks bitten out of them. Painted Lady butterflies, migrating north each year, often arrive tattered and faded after their long journey. The bright, shiny, new Painted Ladies that soon appear probably hatched on thistles in a neglected corner of the yard or from the tangled vegetation of a vacant lot nearby. Such locations are ideal butterfly preserves.

Longer-lived butterflies that hibernate over the winter, such as Mourning Cloaks and Anglewings, may emerge in spring looking rather the worse for wear. These butterflies quickly search for mates and lay their eggs to complete their life cycles before they die.

It is remarkable how such delicate creatures manage to survive wind, weather, and predators at all. This Lorquin's Admiral illustrates how butterflies suffer wing injuries as they age.

Identifying a particular butterfly in your back yard is not always as easy as comparing it to a photograph, even if it does cooperate

Lorquin's Admiral larvae

Lorquin's Admiral, upperwing, with chunk bitten out of wing, on oregano

by posing for the comparison. Even when you have identified a particular butterfly, it may not look exactly the same next time you see it. Butterflies may vary in appearance in different geographical areas or seasons of the year. Earlier generations of butterflies can be lighter or darker than later generations, or even have distinctly different markings. For example, some first-generation Spring Azures display a dark spot in the middle of the underside of the hind wing which does not appear on later spring and summer generations of the species. Males and females of the same kind of butterfly can be identical in appearance or may be very different in colour, size, and markings. Some female "blue" butterflies are quite brown, while the males are

Western Spring Azure

bright, sparkling blue. The female Purplish Copper is bright orange, with dark markings on the upperwings, while her male counterpart displays a distinct purple sheen.

The larvae of butterflies may vary in appearance according to their location and stage of growth. Their appearance usually bears no resemblance to the beautiful adults into which they will metamorphose. Some caterpillars, such as Anise Swallowtail larvae, look like small bird droppings for their first few instars, then become brightly coloured green caterpillars in their later instars. Sometimes the caterpillars are more colourful than the adults they are to become. Banded Woolly Bears, for instance, with their bright black and yellow or black and red furry coats, are well known, while their adult form, the Isabella tiger moth, a dull, mottled amber colour, is less commonly noticed.

Banded Woolly Bear, on red osier dogwood

Lorquin's Admiral • *Limenitis lorquini*

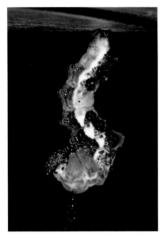

Larva

Pupa

Imago (adult)

Red Admiral • *Vanessa atalanta*

Larva

Pupa

Imago (adult)

White Admiral • *Limenitis arthemis*

Green Anglewing • *Polygonia faunus*

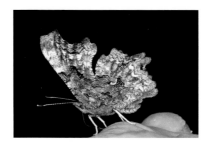

Imagoes (adults)

Satyr Anglewing • *Polygonia satyrus*

Larva

Pupa

Imago (adult)

Zephyr Anglewing • *Polygonia zephyrus*

Imagoes (adults)

Acmon Blue • *Plebejus amon*

Greenish Blue • *Plebejus saepiolus*

Melissa Blue • *Lycaeides melissa*

Silvery Blue • *Glaucopsyche lygdamus*

Larva

Pupa

Imago (adult)

Western Spring Azure • *Celastrina echo*

Two Imagoes (adults) mating

Chalcedon Checkerspot • *Euphydryas chalcedona*

Imago (adult)

Field Cresent • *Phyciodes campestris*

Northern Crescent • *Phyciodes cocyta*

Pale Crescent • *Phyciodes pallida*

Egg mass

Pupa

Larva

Imago (adult)

Common Alpine • *Erebia epipsodea*

Common Ringlet • *Coenonympha*

Pupa   *Larva*

Imagoes (adults)

Mariposa Copper • *Epidemia mariposa*

Pupa

Larva

Imago (adult)

Purplish Copper • *Epidemia helloides*

Brown Elfin • *Incisalia augustinus*

Pupa

Larva

Imago (adult)

Western Pine Elfin • *Incisalia eryphon*

Great Spangled Fritillary • *Speyeria cybele*

Hydaspe Fritillary • *Speyeria hydaspe*

Larva

Pupa

Imago (adult)

Mormon Fritillary • *Speyeria mormonia*

Western Meadow Fritillary • *Boloria epithore*

Zerene Fritillary • *Speyeria zerene*

Two Imagoes (adults) mating

Gray Hairstreak • *Strymon melinus*

Rosner's Hairstreak • *Mitoura rosneri*

Larva

Imago (adult)

Sheridan's Hairstreak • *Callophrys sheridanii*

Painted Lady • *Vanessa cardui*

Larva

Pupa

Imagoes (adults)

West Coast Lady • *Vanessa Anabella*

Large Marble • *Euchole ausonides*

Monarch • *Danaus plexippus*

Larva

Pupa

Imago (adult)

Mourning Cloak • *Nymphalis antiopa*

Larval mass

Imago (adult)

Sara's Orange Tip • *Anthocharis sara*

Larva

Imagoes (adults)

Clodius Parnassian • *Parnassius clodius*

Pupa   *Larva*

Imago (adult)

Arctic Skipper • *Carterocephalus palaemon*

Silver Spotted Skipper • *Epargyreus clarus*

Woodland Skipper • *Ochlodes sylvanoides*

Clouded Sulphur • *Colias philodice*

Anise Swallowtail • *Papilio zelicaon*

Larva 3rd instar

Pupa (top) and larva

Imago (adult)

Canadian Tiger Swallowtail • *Papilio canadensis*

Oregon Tiger Swallowtail • *Papilio bairdii ssp. oregonius*

Pale Tiger Swallowtail • *Papilio eurymedon*

Pupa

Larva

Imago (adult)

Two-Tailed Swallowtail • *Papilio mulitcaudatus*

Western Tiger Swallowtail • *Papilio rutulus*

Compton Tortoiseshell • *Nymphalis vaualbum*

Milbert's Tortoiseshell • *Nymphalis milbert*

Pupa

Larva

Imago (adult)

Cabbage White • *Pieris rapae*

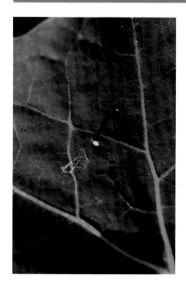

Larva

Egg on nasturtium leaf

Imago (adult)

Margined White • *Pieris marginalis*

Two Imagoes (adults) mating

Pine White • *Neophasia menapia*

Western White • *Pontia occidentalis*

Common Wood Nymph • *Cercyonis pegala*

Pupa

Larva

Imago (adult)

Small Wood Nymph • *Cercyonis oetus*

Climate Zone Map

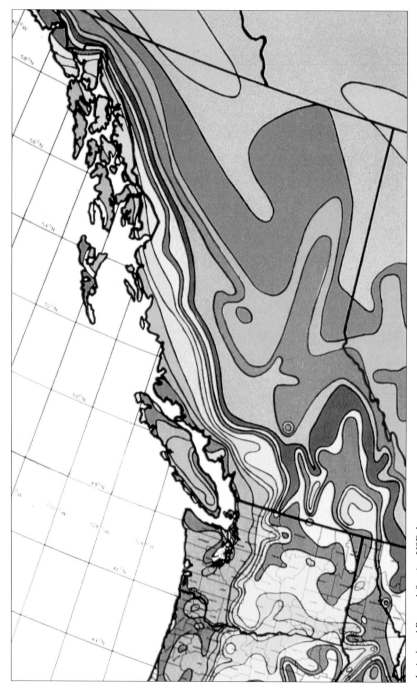

Agricultural Research Service, USDA

AVERAGE ANNUAL MINIMUM TEMPERATURE

Temperature (°C)	Zone	Temperature (°F)
-45.6 and Below	1	Below -50
-42.8 to -45.5	2a	-45 to -50
-40.0 to -42.7	2b	-40 to -45
-37.3 to -40.0	3a	-35 to -40
-34.5 to -37.2	3b	-30 to -35
-31.7 to -34.4	4a	-25 to -30
-28.9 to -31.6	4b	-20 to -25
-26.2 to -28.8	5a	-15 to -20
-23.4 to -26.1	5b	-10 to -15
-20.6 to -23.3	6a	-5 to -10
-17.8 to -20.5	6b	0 to -5
-15.0 to -17.7	7a	5 to 0
-12.3 to -15.0	7b	10 to 5
-9.5 to -12.2	8a	15 to 10
-6.7 to -9.4	8b	20 to 15
-3.9 to -6.6	9a	25 to 20
-1.2 to -3.8	9b	30 to 25
1.6 to -1.1	10a	35 to 30
4.4 to 1.7	10b	40 to 35
4.5 and Above	11	40 and Above

Larval Host Plants

TREES	ZONE	TALL	MEDIUM	LOW	SPRING	SUMMER	FALL	BUTTERFLY LARVAE
Alder (*Alnus*)	all	•	•	•	•	•	•	Pale Tiger Swallowtail, GreenComma, Canadian Tiger Swallowtail
Apple (*Malus*)	to 2	•	•	•	•	•		Western Tiger Swallowtail
Arbutus (*Arbutus*)	7-10	•			•	•		Western or Brown Elfin
Ash (*Fraxinus*)	to 2	•	•	•	•			Two-tailed Swallowtail
Aspen (*Populus*)	to 2	•			•	•		Western Tiger Swallowtail, White Admiral, Canadian Tiger Swallowtail
Birch (*Betula*)	all	•	•	•	•	•	•	Compton Tortoiseshell, Mourning Cloak, Green Comma, Canadian Tiger Swallowtail
Cherry (*Prunus*)	all	•	•	•	•	•		Western Spring Azure
Choke Cherry (*Prunus virginiana*)								Two-tailed Swallowtail, Striped Hairstreak
Dogwood (*Cornus*)	2-8	•	•	•	•			Spring Azure
Elm (*Ulmus*)	to 3	•			•	•	•	Mourning Cloak
Hawthorn (*Crataegu*s)	to 2	•	•		•	•		White Admiral
Pine (*Pinus*)	to 2	•	•		•	•	•	Pine White, Western Pine Elfin
Poplar (*Populus*)	to 2	•			•	•	•	Lorquin's Admiral, Mourning Cloak, Western Tiger Swallowtail, Canadian Tiger Swallowtail
Western Red cedar (*Thuja plicata*)	5-10	•				•	•	Rosner's Hairstreak
Willow (*Salix*)	to 2	•	•	•	•	•	•	Lourquin's Admiral, White Admiral, Mourning Cloak, Western Tiger Swallowtail, Canadian Tiger Swallowtail, Compton Tortoiseshell

SHRUBS	ZONE	TALL	MEDIUM	LOW	SPRING	SUMMER	FALL	BUTTERFLY LARVAE
Blueberry (*Vaccinium*)	all		•	•	•	•	•	Northern Blue, Mariposa Copper
Ceanothus (*Ceanothus*)	8-10	•	•	•		•	•	Pale Tiger Swallowtail
Currant (*Ribes*)	all		•	•	•	•	•	Zephyr Anglewing
Hard hack (*Spirea*)			•	•	•	•		Western Spring Azure
Kinnikinnik (*Arctostaphylos*)	to 2			•	•	•		Western or Brown Elfin
Rhododendron (*Rhododendron*)	2-10	•	•		•		•	Zephyr Anglewing
Salal (*Gaultheria*)	6-10		•	•	•	•		Western or Brown Elfin

VINES	ZONE	TALL	MEDIUM	LOW	SPRING	SUMMER	FALL	BUTTERFLY LARVAE
Hop (*Humulus*)	to 2	•			•	•	•	Red Admiral
Nasturtium (*Tropaeolum*)			•	•	•	•	•	Cabbage White
Pea (*Lathyrum*)			•	•	•	•		Silvery Blue, Western Tailed Blue
Vetch (*Vicia*)	all		•	•	•	•		Silvery Blue, Western Tailed Blue

HERBACEOUS PLANTS	ZONE	TALL	MEDIUM	LOW	SPRING	SUMMER	FALL	BUTTERFLY LARVAE
Alfafa (*Medicago*)			•		•	•	•	Clouded Sulphur, Orange Sulphur
Angelica (*Angelica*)	to 3	•			•	•	•	Anise Swallowtail
Aster (*Aster*)	2-10	•	•	•	•	•	•	Northern Crescent
Borage (*Borago*)		•				•	•	Painted Lady
Burdock (*Arctium*)	all	•			•	•	•	Painted Lady
Butterfly Weed (*Asclepias*)	3-10	•			•	•	•	Monarch
Cabbage (*Brassica*)			•	•	•	•	•	Cabbage White
Clover (*Melilotus/Trifolium*)	all	•	•	•	•	•	•	Clouded Sulpher, Orange Sulpher, Greenish Blue
Cow Parsnip (*Heracleum*)	to 2	•			•	•	•	Anise Swallowtail
Docks (*Rumex*)	all	•	•		•	•	•	Purplish Copper
Fireweed (*Epilobium*)	all	•	•			•	•	Bedstraw Sphinx Moth
Grass	all	•	•	•	•	•	•	Common Alpine, Arctic Skipper, Common Woodnymph, Common Ringlet
Hollyhock (*Alcea*)	to 2	•			•	•	•	West Coast Lady
Knotweed (*Polygonum*)	to 2	•	•	•	•	•	•	Purplish Copper
Lupine (*Lupinus*)	all	•	•	•	•	•		Silvery Blue
Mallow (*Sidalcea/Alcea*)	to 2	•			•	•	•	West Coast Lady
Mustard (*Cruciferae*)	all	•	•	•	•	•	•	Cabbage White, Sara's Orange Tip, Margined White, Western White
Parsley (*Petroselinum*)	to 2		•	•	•	•	•	Anise Swallowtail
Queen Anne's Lace (*Daucus carota*)	all	•			•	•	•	Anise Swallowtail
Rockcress (*Arabis*)								Becker's White
Stinging Nettle (*Urtica dioica*)	all	•	•		•	•	•	Red Admiral, Painted Lady, West Coast Lady, Milbert's Tortoiseshell
Tarragon (*Aremesia Dracunculus*)	to 2	•			•	•	•	Oregon Tiger Swallowtail
Thistle (*Cirsium*)	all	•			•	•	•	Painted Lady
Violet (*Viola*)	to 2		•	•	•	•	•	Great Spangled, Mormon, Western Meadow, Zerene, Hydaspe Fritillaries

Food Sources for Adult Butterflies

TREES	ZONE	TALL	MEDIUM	LOW	SPRING	SUMMER	FALL	FOOD SOURCE
Alder (*Alnus*)	all	•	•	•	•	•	•	tree sap
Apple (*Malus*)	to 2	•	•	•	•	•	•	blossom nectar, rotting fruit, tree sap
Arbutus (*Arbutus*)	7-10	•		•				blossom nectar
Aspen (*Populus*)	to 2	•			•	•	•	tree sap
Birch (*Betula*)	all	•	•	•	•	•	•	tree sap
Cherry (*Prunus*)	all	•	•	•	•	•	•	blossom nectar, rotting fruit, tree sap
Plum (*Prunus*)	all	•	•	•	•	•	•	blossom nectar, rotting fruit, tree sap
Pussy Willow *(Salix)*	2-10	•	•					blossom nectar
Willow (*Salix*)	to 2	•	•	•	•	•	•	tree sap

SHRUBS	ZONE	TALL	MEDIUM	LOW	SPRING	SUMMER	FALL	FOOD SOURCE
Butterfly bush (*Buddleia*)	to 5	•	•			•	•	blossom nectar
Cinquefoil *(Potentilla)*	2-8		•			•	•	blossom nectar
Cotoneaster (*Cotoneaster*)	to 2	•	•	•	•			blossom nectar
Firethorn (*Pyracantha*)	6-10	•	•		•			blossom nectar
Fuchsia *(fuchsia)*	6-10	•			•	•	•	blossom nectar
Honeysuckle (*Lonicera*)	2-9	•	•		•	•		blossom nectar
Lilac (*Syringa*)	3-7	•	•	•	•			blossom nectar
Mock Orange (*Philadelphus*)	4-8	•	•		•			blossom nectar
Rose (*Rosa*)	2-10	•	•	•	•	•	•	blossom nectar
Salmonberry *(Rubus)*	7-10	•			•	•		blossom nectar, rotting fruit
Saskatoonberry (*Amelanchier*)	2-10	•	•		•	•		blossom nectar, rotting fruit
Wiegela (*Wiegela*)	4-8	•	•			•		blossom nectar

VINES	ZONE	TALL	MEDIUM	LOW	SPRING	SUMMER	FALL	FOOD SOURCE
Blackberry (*Rubus*)	2-9	•	•	•			•	blossom nectar, rotting fruit
Honeysuckle (*Lonicera*)	2-9	•	•		•	•		blossom nectar
Wisteria (*Wisteria*)	5-10	•		•				blossom nectar

Tall Herbaceous Plants: Annual, Biennial or Perennial

PLANT NAME	ZONE	TALL	MEDIUM	LOW	SPRING	SUMMER	FALL	
Angelica (*Angelica*)	to 3	•			•	•		Biennial/Perennial
Bee balm (*Monarda*)	to 2	•			•	•		Perennial
Borage (*Borago*)		•			•	•		Annual
Butterfly weed (*Asclepias*)	3-10	•	•		•			Perennial
Chrysanthemum (*Chrysanthemum*)	to 2	•	•			•	•	Annual/Perennial
Clover (*Melilotus/Trifolium*)	all	•	•	•	•	•	•	Perennial
Coreopsis (*Coreopsis*)	all	•	•	•	•			Annual/Perennial
Cranesbill Geranium (*Geranium*)	to 2	•	•		•	•		Perennial
Day Lily (*Hemerocallis*)	to 2	•	•		•	•		Perennial
Delphinium (*Delphinium*)	to 2	•	•		•	•		Perennial
Evening Primrose (*Oenothera*)	to 2	•	•	•	•			Biennial/Perennial
Fireweed (*Epilobium*)	all	•			•	•		Perennial
Gay Feather (*Liatris*)	to 2	•			•	•		Perennial
Gloriosa daisy (*Rudbeckia*)	to 3	•			•	•		Biennial/Perennial
Goldenrod (*Solidago*)	all	•	•	•	•	•		Perennial
Hollyhocks (*Alcea*)	to 2	•			•	•	•	Biennial/Perennial
Jacob's Ladder (*Polemonium*)	to 2	•			•			Perennial
Joe Pye Weed (*Eupatorium*)	to 3	•				•	•	Perennial
Knotweed (*Polygonum*)	to 2	•	•	•	•	•		Perennial
Lantana (*Lantana*)	to 8	•			•	•		Perennial
Lavender (*Lavandula*)	to 4	•	•		•	•		Perennial
Lobelia (*Lobelia*)	to 2	•		•	•	•		Annual/Perennial
Mallow (*Malva/Sidalcea*)	to 2	•	•		•			Biennial/Perennial
Mints (*Mentha*)	to 2	•	•	•	•			Perennial
Money Plant (*Lunaria*)	to 2	•	•		•			Annual/Biennial
Monkshood (*Aconitum*)	to 2	•				•	•	Perennial
Mulleins (*Verbascum*)	to 2	•				•	•	Biennial
Mustards (*Cruciferae*)	all	•	•	•	•	•	•	Annual, Biennial or Perennial
Nasturtium (*Tropaeolum*)			•			•	•	Annual
Onion (*Allium*)	to 3	•	•	•	•	•		Perennial
Phlox (*Phlox*)	to 2	•	•	•	•	•		Perennial
Purple Cone Flower (*Echinacea*)	2-10	•				•	•	Perennial
Queen Anne's Lace (*Daucus carota*)	all	•	•			•	•	Perennial
Red Valerian (*Centranthus*)	to 4	•			•	•		Perennial
Rosemary (*Rosmarinus*)	to 7	•	•		•			Perennial
Shasta daisy (*Chrysanthemum*)	to 2	•			•			Perennial
Sweet Rocket (*Hesperis*)	to 2	•	•		•			Perennial
Thistle (*Cirsium*)	all	•				•	•	Perennial
Valerian (*Valeriana*)	all	•				•		Perennial

Medium Herbaceous Plants: Annual, Biennial or Perennial

PLANT NAME	ZONE	TALL	MEDIUM	LOW	SPRING	SUMMER	FALL	
Alfalfa (*Medicago*)			•		•	•	•	Annual
Alyssum (*Lobularia*)				•	•	•	•	Annual
Aster (*Aster*)	2-10	•	•			•	•	Perennial
Bluebell (*Mertensia*)	to 2	•	•		•			Perennial
Butterfly weed (*Asclepias*)	3-10	•	•			•		Perennial
Calendula (*Calendula*)			•			•	•	Annual
Candytuft (*Iberis*)	to 6		•	•	•	•	•	Perennial or annual
Carnation (*Dianthus*)	to 2	•	•		•	•		Perennial or annual
Chive (*Allium*)	to 2		•	•	•			Perennial
Chrysanthemum (*Chrysanthemum*)	to 2	•	•			•		Perennial
Clover (*Melilotus/Trifolium*)	to 2	•	•	•	•	•	•	Perennial
Columbine (*Aquilegia*)	to 2	•			•	•		Perennial
Coreopsis (*Coreopsis*)	to 2	•	•	•		•	•	Perennial/Annual
Cornflower (*Centaurea*)			•			•		Annual
Cranesbill Geranium (*Geranium*)	to 2	•	•		•	•		Perennial
Cress (*Arabis*)	all		•	•				Perennial
Dandelion (*Taraxacum*)	all		•	•	•			Perennial
Day Lily (*Hermerocallis*)	to 2	•	•			•		Perennial
English Daisy (*Bellis perennis*)			•	•	•			Perennial
Evening Primrose (*Oenothera*)	to 2	•	•	•		•		Biennial/Perennial
Goldenrod (*Solidago*)	all	•	•	•		•	•	Perennial
Hawkweed (*Hieracium*)	all	•				•	•	Perennial
Knotweed (*Polygonum*)	to 2	•	•	•		•	•	Perennial
Lantana (*Lantana*)	to 8	•	•	•		•	•	Perennial or Annual
Lavender (*Lavandula*)	to 4	•	•		•	•	•	Perennial
Lobelia (*Lobelia*)	to 2	•		•		•	•	Perennial or Annual
Lungwort (*Pulmonaria*)	to 2	•	•	•				Perennial
Mallow (*Malva Sidalcea*)	to 2	•	•			•		Biennial/Perennial
Mint(*Mentha*)	to 2	•	•	•		•		Perennial
Money Plant (*Lunaria*)	to 2	•	•		•			Annual or Biennial
Mustard (*Cruciferae*)	all	•	•	•	•	•	•	Annual, Biennial or Perennial
Nasturtium (*Tropaeolum*)			•	•		•	•	Annual
Onion (*Allium*)	to 3	•	•	•	•	•		Perennial
Oregano (*Origanum*)	to 4	•				•		Perennial
Pearly Everlasting (*Anaphalis*)	all	•				•	•	Perennial

continued, next page>

PLANT NAME	ZONE	TALL	MEDIUM	LOW	SPRING	SUMMER	FALL	
Phlox (*Phlox*)	to 2	•	•	•	•	•		Perennial
Pinkweed (*Polygonum*)	to 2		•		•	•		Perennial
Queen Anne's Lace (*Daucus carota*)	all	•	•			•	•	Perennial
Rosemary (*Rosemarinus*)	to 7	•	•		•			Perennial
Speedwell (*Veronica*)	to 4	•	•		•			Perennial
Stonecrop (*Sedum*)	2-10		•		•	•		Perennial
Sweet Rocket (*Hesperis*)	to 2	•	•	•	•			Perennial
Sweet William (*Dianthus*)	to 2		•		•			Biennial
Thyme (*Thymus*)	to 4		•		•			Perennial
Verbena (*Verbena*)	to 5		•	•	•			Perennial
Vetch (*Vicia*)	all		•		•	•		Perennial
Wallflower (*Cheiranthus*)	to 5		•	•	•			Biennial/Perennial
Wood Sorrel (*Oxalis*)	to 3		•	•	•	•		Perennial
Yarrow (*Achillea*)	all	•	•		•	•		Perennial
Zinnia (*Zinnia*)		•	•		•	•		Annual

Purple Cone Flower

Alder

Alfalfa

Alsike Clover

Angelica

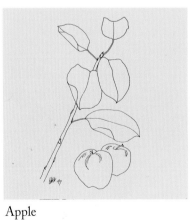

Apple

Arbutus

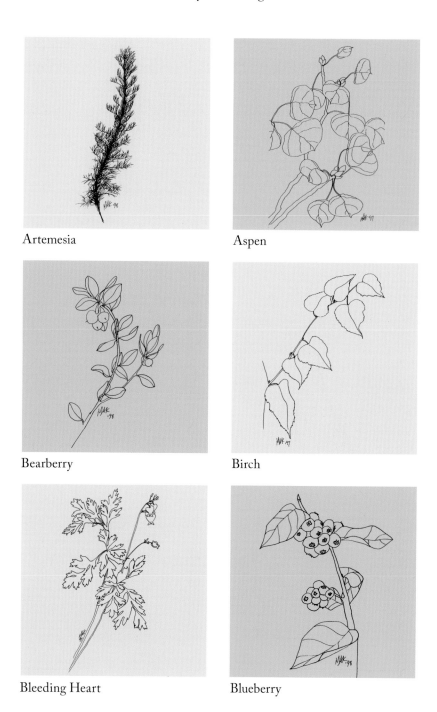

Artemesia

Aspen

Bearberry

Birch

Bleeding Heart

Blueberry

Cow Parsnip

Curled Dock

Currant

Dogwood

Fireweed

Hardhack

Hawthorn

Holly

Hollyhock

Honeysuckle

Hops

Knotweed

Lupine

Mountain Ash

Mustard

Nasturtium

Oak

Parsley

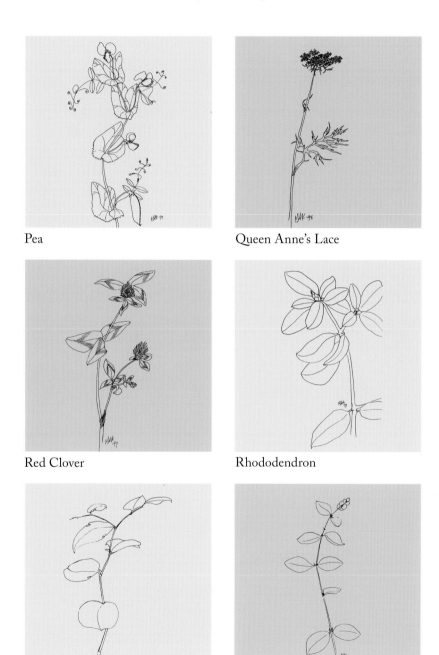

Pea

Queen Anne's Lace

Red Clover

Rhododendron

Salal

Snowberry

Stinging Nettle

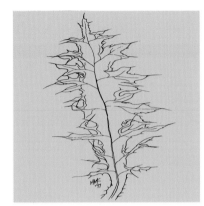

Thistle

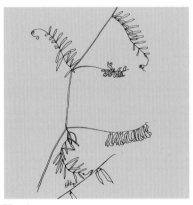

Vetch

Violet

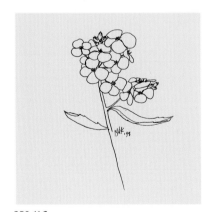

Wallflower

Willow

Sources of Plants and Seeds

Cultivated plants are available at any nursery. It can be more difficult to find wild and heritage varieties (such as the old-fashioned, single-flowering versions of hollyhock). Some nurseries stock heritage varieties of plants and their seeds. Some seed catalogues carry or specialize in heritage plants or wild plants. The Internet is a great resource for hard-to-find plants and seeds. Other good sources are seed-saver societies. These may be contacted through botanical gardens like Van Dusen Gardens in Vancouver. The University of British Columbia's botanical garden shop also offers less common plants and seeds. Garden clubs are another wonderful source of information, seeds, and plants. Many gardening magazines advertise nurseries, detailing the kinds of plants that are their specialties.

Silver Blue, male

British Columbia

**Art's Nursery Wholesale &
Retail**
8940 - 192nd Street
Surrey BC V3A 4P9
Mailing Address:
8875 Armstrong Road RR 6
Langley BC V1M 2R3
ph: (604) 882-1201
fax: (604) 882-5969

Aurora Farm
3492 Phillips Road
Creston BC V0B 1G2
ph: (250) 428-4404
aurora@kootenay.com
www.kootenay.com/~aurora/

BC's Wild Heritage Plants
47330 Extrom Road
Chilliwack BC V2R 4V1
ph: (604) 858-5141
bcwild@uniserve.com

Bluestem Nursery
1949 Fife Road
Mission BC V2V 5X4
ph: (604) 820-0845
fax: (604) 820-0845

Butchart Gardens
PO Box 4010
Victoria BC V8X 3X4
email@butchartgardens.com
www.butchartgardens.com

**C.E. Jones & Associates Ltd.
Native Plant Nursery**
204 - 26 Bastion Square
Victoria BC V8W 1H9
ph: (250) 383-8375
fax: (250) 383-9354
blapierre@jonesassoc.com

Dry Valley Gardens
669 Curtis Road
Kelowna BC V1V 2C9
ph: (250) 762-6018
fax: (250) 860-6836

Elysium Garden Nursery
2834 Belgo Road
Kelowna BC V1P 1E2
ph: (250) 491-1368

Fraser's Thimble Farms
175 Arbutus Road
Saltspring Island, BC V8K
1A3
ph: (250) 537-5788
fax: (250) 537-5788
thimble@saltspring.com

Gabriola Growing Co.
RR 1, Site 3CA
Gabriola Island BC V0R 1X0
ph: (250) 247-8204

The Green House
1340 Wain Road
Sidney BC V8L 5V1
ph: (250) 655-4391
fax: (250) 655-9350

Hallman Nurseries
200 Old Divide Road,
Ganges
Salt Spring Island BC
V8K 2G7
ph: (250) 537-9316

Jones Nurseries Ltd.
16880 Westminster Highway
Richmond BC V6V 1A8
ph: (604) 278-0078
fax: (604) 273-0650
inquiry@jonesnurseries.com
www.jonesnurseries.com

Manhattan Farms
3088 Salmon River Road
Salmon Arm BC V1E 4M1
ph: (604) 379-2800

Mayo Creek Gardens
6596 McLean Road, Box 351
Lake Cowichan BC V0R 2G0
ph: (250) 749-6291
fax: (250) 749-4298

Meadowsweet Farms
24640 16th Avenue
Langley BC V2Z 1J4
ph: (604) 530-2611
fax: (604) 530-9996

**Minter Country Garden
Store & Nursery**
10015 Young Street North
Chilliwack BC V2P 4V3
ph: 1-800-661-3919
www.mintergardens.com/
country. htm

Mosswood Perennials
451 Creed Road, RR 6
Victoria BC V9E 1C6
ph: (250) 474-3322

NATS Nursery Ltd.
24555 32nd Avenue
Langley BC V2Z 2J5
ph: (604) 530-9300
fax: (604 530-9500
www.natsnaturals.com
(retail)
www.natsnursery.com
(wholesale)

Nature's Garden Seed Co.
PO Box 40121
905 Gordon Street
Victoria BC V8W 3N3
ph: (250) 595-2062
fax: (250) 595-2062

Okanagan Natural Habitats
825 DeHart Road
Kelowna BC V1W 4N2
ph: (250) 764-8899
fax: (250) 764-2908

Pacific Rim Native Plants
44305 Old Orchard Road
Sardis BC V2R 1A9
ph: (604) 792-9279
fax: (604) 792-1891

The Perennial Garden Inc.
13139 224th Street
Maple Ridge BC V4R 2P6
ph: (604) 467-4218
fax: (604) 467-3181
www.perennialgardener.com

**Petals & Butterflies Farm
Nursery**
121 - 210 Street (off 0 Avenue)
Langley BC V2Z 2G6
ph: (604) 530-9205
petalsandbutterflies@shaw.ca

Rain Forest Nurseries Inc.
1470 - 227th Street
Langley BC V5A 6H5
ph: (604) 530-3499
fax: (604) 530-3499

R & M Nursery
SS2 C6 S13
[8703 - 100th Avenue]
Fort St. John BC V1J 4M7
ph: (250) 785-5296
fax: (250) 785-5296

Sagebrush Nursery
38084 - 93rd Street (Island
Road), Oliver BC
Mailing Address:
RR 2 S14 C11
Oliver BC V0H 1T0
ph: (250) 498-8898 or
1-800-467-6111
fax: (250) 498-8892

Streamside Native Plants
3300 Fraser Road
RR 6 S695 C6
Courtenay BC V9N 8H9
ph: (250) 338-7509
fax: (250) 338-7509
barport@mars.ark.com

**Summerland Ornamental
Gardens**
ph: (250) 494-6385

Sunrise Cactus Gardens
No. 75, Highway 3A
Keremeos BC V0X 1N0
ph: (250) 499-5105

**University of BC Botanical
Garden Shop in the Garden**
6804 SW Marine Drive
Vancouver BC V6T 1Z4
ph: (604) 822-4529
www.ubcbotanicalgarden.org

VanDusen Botanical Garden
5251 Oak Street (at 37th
Avenue)
Vancouver BC V6M 4H1
ph: (604) 878-9274
fax: (604) 266-4236
www.vandusengarden.org

**Woodland Native Plant
Nursery**
4060 Happy Valley Road
Victoria BC V9B 5T7
ph: (250) 478-6084
fax: (250) 478-6084

Alberta

Alberta Nurseries & Seeds
PO Box 20
Bowden AB T0M 0K0
ph: (403) 224-3544
fax: (403) 224-2455
dectool@telusplanet.net

**ALCLA Native Plant
Restoration**
3208 Bearspaw Drive NW
Calgary AB T2L 1T2
ph: (403) 282-6516
fax: (403) 282-7090
fedkenhp@cadvision.com
www.alclanativeplants.com

**Blazing Star Wildflower Seed
Company**
PO Box 1496
Didsbury AB T0M 0W0
ph: (403) 335-4956
fax: (403) 335-9482
seeds@growwildflowers.com
www.growwildflowers.com

Bow Point Nursery
244034 Range Road 32
Calgary AB T3Z 2E3
ph: (403) 686-4434
fax: (403) 242-8018
bowpoint@agt.net

Devonian Botanic Garden
Friends of the Garden
University of Alberta
Edmonton AB T6G 2E1
ph: (780) 987-3054
fax: (780) 987-4141
www.discoveredmonton.com/
devonian/dbg.html

Enviro Scapes
PO Box 38
Warner AB T0K 2L0
ph: (403) 733-2160
fax: (403) 733-2161
enscapes@telusplanaet.net

**Grumpy's Greenhouses &
Gardens Ltd.**
PO Box 2488
Pincher Creek AB T0K 1W0
ph: (403) 627-4589
fax: (403) 627-2909
grumpys@telusplanet.net

Canada

Native Plant Society of BC
2012 William Street
Vancouver BC V5L 2X6
information@npsbc.org
www.npsbc.org

Seeds of Diversity Canada
PO Box 36, Station Q
Toronto ON M4T 2L7
ph: (905) 623-0353
mail@seeds.ca
www.seeds.ca

Victoria Horticultural Society
PO Box 5081, Postal Station B
Victoria BC V8R 6N3
ph: (250) 381-4078
cmb@islandnet.com

Washington

**Abundant Seed Life
Foundation**
PO Box 772
Port Townsend WA 98386
ph: (360) 385-5660
fax: (360) 385-7455
abundant@olypen.com

Briggs Nursery
4407 Henderson Boulevard
Olympia WA 98501
ph: (360) 352-5405
www.briggsnursery.com

Cloud Mountain Farm
6906 Goodwin Road
Everson WA 98247
ph: (360) 966-5859
fax: (360) 966-0921
info@cloudmountainfarm.com
www.cloudmountainfarm.com

Green Man Gardens
Mercer Island WA
ph: (206) 232-5734
bnbjohns@home.com

Hillview Gardens Products
5404 West Metaline Avenue
Kennewick WA 99336
ph: (509) 783-2695

Lawyer Nursery
7515 Meridian Road SE
Olympia WA 98503
ph: (800) 551-9875
seeds@lawyernursery.com
www.lawyernursery.com

Pacific Natives and Ornamentals
PO Box 23
Bothell WA 98041
ph: (206) 483-9108
fax: (206) 487-6198

Sound Native Plants
PO Box 7505
Olympia WA 98507
ph: (360) 352-4122
fax: (360) 867-0007
joslyn@www.soundnativeplants.com
www.soundnativeplants.com

Viewcrest Nurseries
12713 NE 184 Street
Battle Ground WA 98604
ph: (360) 687-5167
fax: (360) 687-1212
bamboo@viewcrest.com
www.viewcrest.com

Washington Native Plant Society
6310 NE 74th Street Suite 215E
Seattle WA 98115
ph: (206) 527-3210 or
1-888-288-8022
wnps@blarg.net
www.wnps.org

Woodbrook Nursery
5919 78th Avenue NW
Gig Harbor WA 98335
ph: (253) 265-6271
fax: (253) 265-6461

Oregon

Boskey Dell Natives
23311 SW Boskey Dell Lane
West Linn OR 97068
ph: (503) 638-5945

Down to Earth
532 Olive Street
Eugene OR 97401
ph: (541) 342-6820
fax: (541) 342-2261

Forestfarm
990 Tetherow Road
Williams OR 97544-9599
ph: (541) 846-7269
fax: (541) 846-6963
plants@forestfarm.com
www.forestfarm.com

Hansen Nursery
PO Box 1228
North Bend OR 97459
ph: (541) 756-1156

Oakhill Farms
4314 Goodrich Highway
Oakland OR 97462-9636
ph: (541) 459-1361

Wallace Hansen, Native Plants of the Northwest
2158 Bower Court SE
Salem OR 97301
ph: (503) 581-2638
fax: (503) 581-9957
plants@nwplants.com
www.nwplants.com

Alaska

Alaska Botanical Garden
PO Box 202202
Anchorage AK 99520
ph: (907) 770-3692
fax: (907) 770-0555
garden@alaskabg.org
http://www.alaskabg.org/

Alaska Native Plant Nursery
Nancy Moore, Manager
Trunk Spur Road
HC 01 Box 6150
Palmer AK 99645
ph: (907) 746-7241
fax: (907) 746-7261
Nancy_Moore@dnr.state.ak.us

Bush Landscaping & Nursery
2848 Lore Road
Anchorage AK 99507
ph: (907) 344-2775
fax: (907) 349-4507
Peggie Reynolds

Landscape Alaska
PO Box 32654
Juneau AK 99803
ph: (907) 790-4916
www.landscapealaska.com
David Lendrum

Seeds of Alaska
PO Box 3127
48535 Cardwell Road
Kenai AK 99611
ph: (907) 260-1980
fax: (907) 260-1977
seeds@ptialaska.net
Dick Baldwin

California

California Native Plant Society
2707 K Street, Suite 1
Sacramento CA 95816-5113
ph: (916) 447-2677
fax: (916) 447-2727
cnps@cnps.org
www.cnps.org/index.htm

El Nativo Growers, Inc.
ph: (626) 969-8449
fax: (626) 969-7299
sales@elnativogrowers.com
www.elnativogrowers.com

Las Pilitas Nursery
3232 Las Pilitas Road
Santa Margarita CA 93453
ph: (805) 438-5992
www.laspilitas.com/

San Francisco Bay Wildlife Society
PO Box 524
Newark CA 94560-0524
ph: (510) 792-4275
fax: (510) 792-5828
www.sfbws.org

Glossary

Annual: plant living only one growing season

Biennial: plant taking two years to mature, flowering and dying the second year

Larval: host plant—plant on which larvae feed

Imago: adult butterfly

Instar: a caterpillar's growth period between molts

Larva: caterpillar

Osmeterium: a retractable growth in a caterpillar's head

Perennial: plant living several to many years

Proboscis: tube that is the butterfly's mouth

Pupa: chrysalis, the stage beween caterpillar and adult

Weed: any plant growing where someone does not want it to grow

Index of Common Names

Acmon Blue / *Plebejus amon*, 50

Anise Swallowtail / *Papilio zelicaon*, 39, 73

Arctic Skipper / *Carterocephalus palaemon*, 71

Brown Elfin / *Incisalia augustinus*, 58

Cabbage White / *Pieris rapae*, 79

Canadian Tiger Swallowtail / *Papilio canadensis*, 74

Chalcedon Checkerspot / *Euphydryas chalcedona*, 53

Clodius Parnassian / *Parnassius clodius*, 70

Clouded Sulphur / *Colias philodice*, 72

Common Alpine / *Erebia epipsodea*, 56

Common Ringlet / *Coenonympha*, 56

Common Wood Nymph / *Cercyonis pegala*, 82

Compton Tortoiseshell / *Nymphalis vaualbum*, 77

Field Crescent / *Phyciodes campestris*, 54

Gray Hairstreak / *Strymon melinus*, 62

Great Spangled Fritillary / *Speyeria cybele*, 59

Green Anglewing / *Polygonia faunus*, 48

Greenish Blue / *Plebejus saepiolus*, 51

Hydaspe Fritillary / *Speyeria hydaspe*, 60

Large Marble / *Euchole ausonides*, 66

Lorquin's Admiral / *Limenitis lorquini*, 46

Margined White / *Pieris marginalis*, 80

Mariposa Copper / *Epidemia mariposa*, 57

Melissa Blue / *Lycaeides melissa*, 51

Milbert's Tortoiseshell / *Nymphalis milbert*, 78

Monarch / *Danaus plexippus*, 67

Mormon Fritillary / *Speyeria mormonia*, 61

Mourning Cloak / *Nymphalis antiopa*, 68

Northern Crescent / *Phyciodes cocyta*, 54

Oregon Tiger Swallowtail / *Papilio bairdii Ssp. oregonius*, 74

Painted Lady / *Vanessa cardui*, 65

Pale Crescent / *Phyciodes pallida*, 55

Pale Tiger Swallowtail / *Papilio eurymedon*, 75

Pine White / *Neophasia menapia*, 81

Purplish Copper / *Epidemia helloides*, 58

Red Admiral / *Vanessa atalanta*, 47

Rosner's Hairstreak / *Mitoura rosneri*, 63

Sara's Orange Tip / *Anthocharis sara*, 69

Satyr Anglewing / *Polygonia satyrus*, 49

Sheridan's Hairstreak / *Callophrys sheridanii*, 64

Silvery Blue / *Glaucopsyche lygdamus*, 52

Silver Spotted Skipper / *Epargyreus clarus*, 71

Small Wood Nymph / *Cercyonis oetus*, 83

Two-Tailed Swallowtail / *Papilio mulitcaudatus*, 76

West Coast Lady, *Vanessa Anabella*, 66

Western Meadow Fritillary / *Boloria epithore*, 61

Western Pine Elfin / *Incisalia eryphon*, 59

Western Spring Azure / *Celastrina echo*, 53

Western Tiger Swallowtail / *Papilio rutulus*, 77

Western White / *Pontia beckerii*, 81

White Admiral / *Limenitis arthemis*, 48

Woodland Skipper / *Ochlodes sylvanoides*, 72

Zephyr Anglewing / *Polygonia zephyrus*, 50

Zerene Fritillary / *Speyeria zerene*, 62